TRAVEL LIKE AN ARCHITECT

The Basics

C. Evan H.

Disclaimer: This book is full of my thoughts and opinions which should not be taken as fact or law.

Paperback ISBN: 978-1-7377328-1-5
Ebook ISBN: 978-1-7377328-0-8

Library of Congress Control Number: 2021916375

First paperback edition August 2021

Edited by Kensi Bui
Illustrated by C. Evan H.
Cover art by C. Evan H.
Layout by C. Evan H.

Printed by Kindle Direct Publishing

Author Website: cevanh.myportfolio.com

Dedicated to those who love to find the everyday stories in life

TABLE OF CONTENTS

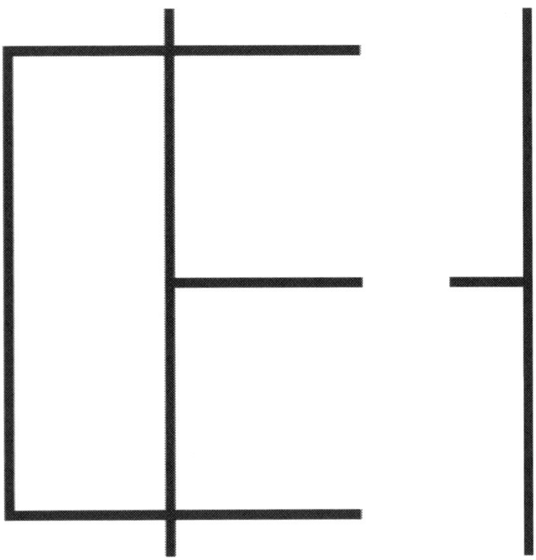

INTRODUCTION

I do not claim to speak on behalf of the entire architectural community, nor would I wish to be proclaimed as their representative. Architects vary in personality and world outlook just as much as any other career field in society. So, when I say "Travel like an Architect," understand that I refer to the type of architect I am. Take heed now, for I am unapologetically and unequivocally myself, dear reader.

I started architecture school in the Fall of 2016 and wrapped up my Master of Architecture degree in the Spring of 2021. Needless to say, the world has changed quite a bit in that time frame, and I grew hand-and-hand alongside it, still in some ways coping with the lessons I've learned.

But that's the point of life, is it not? To learn lessons? No one should fear the thought of learning lessons, though, because at its core, that's the point of traveling as well. Some travel to learn about other cultures; others travel learn more about those close to them; still more travel to learn new things about themselves.

Yet, learning can be an intimidating idea as the word conjures up memories of high school study guides and pop quizzes for many people. Instead, imagine learning from travel to be the same as learning pop-culture, song lyrics, or backgrounds for book characters. Learning should involve passion, not stress, and that comes through choosing what we learn for basically no other reason than just, simply, because.

Having no experience in something can form another barrier to the idea of learning. It's a lot easier to learn more about what we're already comfortable with than to branch out into something new. However, I realized another way to say "lacking experience" is "a challenge." What we do not know is what we are able to learn.

Just as I did earlier with the word "learning," I will offer an alternative analogy to the word "challenge." Don't think of a learning challenge as difficult a devotion to something with which one lacks experience; rather, imagine it like a scavenger hunt or even a game of Clue. Because when one does not know what he/she/they do not know, one becomes a detective solving a mystery of what one needs to learn.

During my time in college, I had the privilege of spending a semester abroad in Rome, Italy. To say I came back home with a different world view would be an understatement. And while I was expecting to learn a lot about architecture, I was still shocked by how much my understanding of the subject was impacted. It would be fair to say that this trip inspired me to write this book, but I also want to note that I ventured to Rome in 2019 just before the 2020 pandemic. Since then, I have also grown to appreciate the little trips across town.

The very foundation of this book rests on the idea that to "Travel like an Architect," one must be willing to learn, to look past the surface and search for a deeper understanding of where he's/she's/they're going and why. Meander with me through an impassioned consciousness of wanderlust and ponder with me why everyone should travel like an architect.

PART ONE

Before the Trip

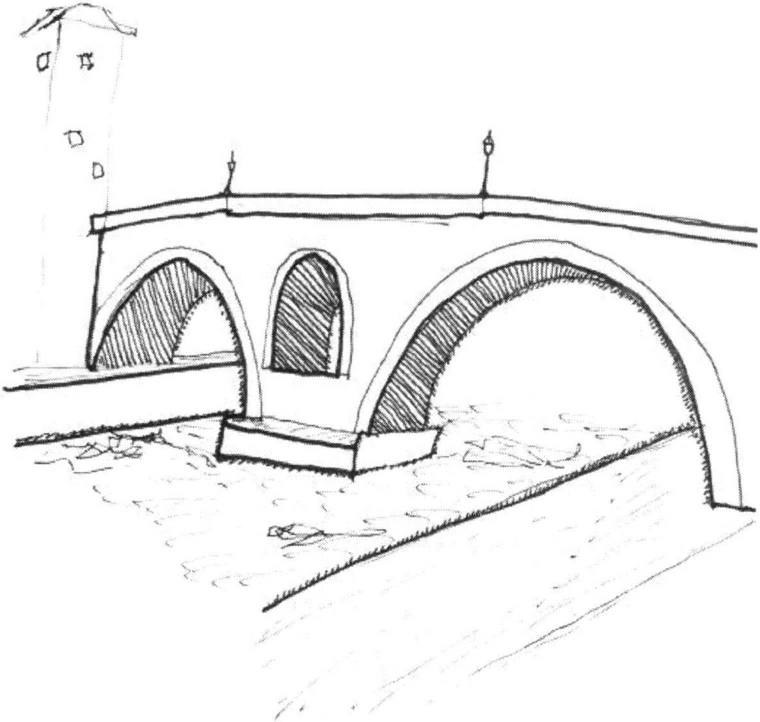

CHOOSING A LOCATION

That old Real Estate cliche, "Location. Location. Location," has become a household phrase in our society and rightfully so, in a sense. Yes, location matters because everybody wants to see something different; however, location simultaneously is unimportant because beauty is in the eye of the beholder. Balancing these two philosophical notions is, as always, the best course of action.

On the one hand, there are the grandiose destination cities like Rome, Paris, New York, Tokyo, etc., and most often the idea of touring great works of architecture conjures up images of these cities. But, the truth is great architecture exists everywhere, just not all of it is famous. I do recommend visiting these cities, yes, but don't assume they are the only outlets for traveling like an architect.

For instance, just a couple streets away from my alma mater, tucked amongst a group of sorority houses, sits a wonderfully outrageous piece of Mid-Twentieth Century residential architecture known as the Ledbetter House, designed by architect Bruce Goff. My travels to this destination include the day my professor just walked us down there for class, as well as the odd days I simply take that street on my commute home and gaze at it as I pass. Easy, so easy.

My point is traveling to see good architecture doesn't have to be expensive, time consuming, or out of reach. More than likely, there's something just around the block you can visit. Seeing the famous buildings everyone talks about and recognizes is a valid way to travel, but planning a trip around the discovery of a niche building online or in a book is no less valid.

Another important concept to keep in mind is that architecture is more than looks. I have often heard that architecture blends the teachings of art and engineering, yet rarely is the concept of behavioral science thrown into that mix. See, architecture has an unambiguous relationship with politics, religions, economics, etc., After all, what is a building if not a permanent billboard used to display some sort of message about who's in charge.

And finding that message really is the fun part of architecture. It's one thing to look and marvel at a building, it's another to listen as walls begin to tell a story. Not to mention, in the case of older buildings, the stories of history fill the space between the walls and either enrichingly harmonize with the story of construction or rather alarmingly counter it.

At this point in our discussion of history, I feel I must clarify that architecture is not limited to just buildings. "The Built Environment" is a catch-all phrase commonly used to discuss architecture in a holistic way, inclusive of buildings, roadways, transportation stations, parks, etc., but even to a city itself. Yes, a city as a whole can be viewed as a piece of architecture no different than an ordinary building would be. Later on, I may use words and phrases like "urban," urbanism" or "the urban scale," which will be used in lieu of this idea of the city as a piece of architecture.

So, when choosing a location to travel based on architecture, keep in mind that the look of the buildings only portray part of the story. Deciding on a destination based on historical events, big or small, and then relating it to the architecture during the visit may be a more fulfilling way to go about it.

PREPARING TO GO

Packing, perhaps, claims the not-so-coveted title of "Most Stressful Part of Preparing for a Trip." Luckily, this chapter isn't about packing at all. Obviously, to travel like an architect, one should pack a small sketchbook and a couple pens or pencils, but that's basically it. So instead, this chapter will focus on the mental preparations needed and getting in the right mindset.

Whether the trip requires a time consuming journey across the world or just a quick drive down the block will determine the stakes of the trip. Is this a once-in-a-lifetime excursion, or will there be an opportunity to go back a few times and uncover mysteries that have been lingering in the back of our minds?

Chapter 2

As mentioned in the previous chapter, knowing the history and stories of a piece of architecture are the keys to understanding and describing it. Therefore, doing a bit of research before embarking would be a big asset when traveling like an architect. Not much is needed, one mustn't feel overwhelmed. Merely a few quick internet articles related to the piece(s) of architecture that influenced the final decision.

Searching for significant events and running amuck down rabbit holes of web-pages is a surprisingly fun way to get hyped for the trip, too. Nothing seems as satisfying as finding a date for a historical event that aligns with one of the days of the trip. And of course, searching for both celebratory and solemn stories is of utmost importance in understanding the lessons of the past. For instance, traveling to Rome deems worthy some research into the opulent splendor of the Catholic cathedrals, but also into the small, golden cobblestones throughout the city marking former homes of the Jews captured in World War II.

No, traveling like an architect doesn't require an advanced degree, nor does it require a full dedication to pure academics; however, it does require a passionate observer with the perseverance to always search for more details to the story.

GETTING THERE

Seemingly every collection of inspirational quotes contains the idea of "it's not the destination; it's the journey." It's not uncommon either for movies or books to portray this idea as the moral to the story. I could not disagree more with this sentiment.

The point of traveling is absolutely, undeniably about the destination, for if a point-B didn't exist, how could there be a journey between it and point-A? No, the destination drums the beating heart of the trip, and all of the planning revolves around the destination, making it unquestionably the focus.

That said, I do still believe the journey to the destination holds great merit. Indeed, in the world of storytelling, the climax makes a bigger impact when more details are added between it and the beginning of the story. Likewise, building a journey to the destination can set the mood for the trip.

But how, of course, can a journey be enjoyable unless the trip is a road trip? Surely, only traveling long distances across many days in a car can provide the opportunity to make worthwhile stops along the way? Incorrect, a dose of creativity is the key to everything fun in life, and traveling is no exception.

Take for example, a trip from somewhere in America to Rome. Naturally, the most time efficient way to get there would be by airplane, and no, I'm not about to suggest taking a boat. Instead, I'm proposing not flying into Rome, but into another Italian city. Which one? Not important. The point is to enter Rome by rail. Hoping off a nine-ish hour flight and then immediately stepping into Rome can be a little overwhelming. But, flying into another Italian city and then taking a train through the Italian countryside into Rome would give the nerves a chance to settle down and soak up the environment before entering the forever bustling eternal city. Plus, stopping in a town or two along the way could incorporate those classic road trip vibes.

Now, on a smaller scale, imagine a simple trip across town or even around the block, one where the journey couldn't possibly be anything more than a 20 minute drive. Well, maybe the journey shouldn't be in the car. Walking is a great way to clear the mind and mentally prepare for just about anything. Alternatively, if it's still necessary to drive to the destination, park a couple blocks away and just take a brief walk. Always keep in mind, arriving at a piece of architecture through the isolation of a car is an entirely different experience than arriving as a pedestrian.

Just as doing some background research over the architecture the trip revolves around provides stories and explanations to why something looks the way it does, so too a journey can reveal the reach of those stories. Often, any of the social or political movements that influence architecture aren't limited to one small area, and understanding whether or not something is or was impressionistic to a society involves seeing how far away it's influence reached.

NOTES

NOTES

PART TWO

During the Trip

ARRIVING AT THE DESTINATION

Here it is, the most exciting part. The destination has been reached, and it feels like the trip has finally started. So fresh, so new, so unexplored; the feeling of accomplishment for actually achieving that goal of traveling is an unrivaled emotion. Arriving marks the transition of preparing to travel and physically exploring the destination.

Upon arrival, the most important thing to do to travel like an architect is to begin thinking with the senses: sight, smell, sound, and feel (I wouldn't, on a normal day, recommend tasting the architecture). And though I've mentioned all architects enjoy different aspects of the profession, sensory observation is a common thread, whether it's a more engineering-impassioned architect finding amusement in the sight of exposed bolted connections of steel beams, or a more socio-political-impassioned architect feeling the bullet holes in a war-stricken ruin. Using the senses is key to understanding architecture.

For urban destinations, the point of arrival is often an airport, a bus or train station, or a city limits sign if traveling by car. Commonly, dropping off baggage at a hotel or other place of sleep is the first stop within the city. Although it may be easy to assume this needs to happen quickly so seeing the city can start, this is the first journey through the city. Therefore, take the opportunity to slow down and absorb the feeling. Hop on the slower train instead of the taxi; get stuck in traffic and play eye-spy with the surroundings; take an early exit and drive through the city streets for a few blocks; or simply take a minute to sit in the airport with a cup of coffee and enjoy the terminal's architecture.

When the destination is a specific building, and whether that's one around the block or across the world, arriving becomes everything that happens before entry. Technically, I want to include the first steps through the door, but saying "before entry" gives more emphasis to the outside. Laying eyes on the building for the first time marks the arrival, which ends at entry.

This also is a good moment to slow down and not rush to get inside. Take a moment to view the facade from different positions, some are meant to be viewed head-on while others at an angle. Note how the building fits with the surroundings, and try to describe it. If one is inexperienced with architectural adjectives, use familiar terminology instead. The building could be light bodied like a glass of wine or perhaps well drafted like a football team.

Not all the learning that takes place on a trip involves research or story hunting. Sometimes, traveling like an architect is just learning to slow down and enjoy the new surroundings, struck by the wonder.

GETTING AROUND

This chapter relates specifically to the scenario where the trip's destination is an urban environment as a whole (i.e. a city). While I have used the word "destination" throughout this book to refer to a multitude of architectural types, I will only be using it to refer to a city in this chapter.

The idea of getting around an urban environment can seem trivial. However, I've already mentioned in chapter 3 that the way in which one arrives at a piece of architecture can affect the experience. That concept came through the discussion of planning a journey to get from the house to the destination. In this chapter, the same concept will be applied to going from one point in the city to another like a series of mini journeys, only these will be unplanned, unscripted, and unrivaled.

Growing up in a car-centric, suburban society, I never developed any kind of imagination for venturing around a city. It was always hop in the car, park as close to the front door to the shop as possible, get in, get out, park in the garage, go back in the house. I remember traveling to New York City for the first time shortly after graduating high school and discovering there wasn't just a single subway that stopped at every station in the city. No, there were multiple lines and it actually mattered which one went where, because not every train went to every station.

Anyway, I tell that anecdote to bring up the idea of getting lost. Sure, it's possible to get lost in a car, but one tends to stay in the car while lost, those lost in public transportation or on foot can have a bit more fun. Yes, I said fun because as someone who has traveled to Rome, I can attest that nothing is more fun than not knowing what lies ahead.

Getting Around

Traveling around a city on a trip should be done on foot as much as possible, with exception to public transit in the case of long distances. Cars should be avoided whenever possible due to their isolation not only from amenities along the street, but also from the public life.

While on foot, it's possible to stumble into a store barely visible in the alley, read a plaque hanging above a historical home, share a laugh with a local when their kid jumps in a big puddle, or even just lean against a wall or bench and people-watch for a few minutes. These are the mini journeys that the point-A-to-point-B purpose of a car can't achieve. Don't confuse seeing the city with visiting a series of landmarks; getting around, moving from place to place is seeing the city.

SEEING THE SIGHTS

As I've previously said, the trip revolves around the destination, so then logically, seeing the sights–the destination(s)–is the climax of traveling. Every bit of planning, every longing look at online pictures, every ounce of anticipation has been leading to this jaw-dropping moment. How, then, can this short time devoted to observing the destination be wisely spent?

The answer is, of course, any way in which one wishes to spend it. Again, there is no one right way to view architecture because everyone looks for something different; everyone finds captivating features in different parts of the whole. And lest it be forgotten, beauty is in the eye of the beholder.

Though the question remains, how can those captivating features be found? After all, they aren't always jumping up and down vying for attention. This goes back to the technique of using the senses to get more information.

First, and most obviously, thoroughly seeing the sights involves looking around, or more accurately gazing at the details. In the case of a building in a city, gazing at any surrounding buildings can reveal more of the story, how they either fit in with or stand out from one another (or sometimes a peculiar mixture of both). For the interior of a building, do the same with the rooms, the walls, the ceilings, the floors, etc. In many ways, the two are the same. Buildings are like rooms within the city and rooms like buildings within a building.

Other details to notice are the materials (e.g. concrete, brick, tile, etc.). Materials do a lot to convey emotion, a key feature in the storytelling. Are they gentle or brutal, grandiose or intimate, playful or serious. Experimenting with some descriptive adjectives is fun for the artists, historians, and engineers alike.

But one of the most impactful--and simultaneously overlooked--contributers to the emotion of architecture is acoustics. I would say acoustics is given it's dues when describing concert halls, but what about libraries, museums, train stations, parks, or even city streets? The sounds within or around a building affect it, too. Take time to notice echoes, flowing fountains, or uninterrupted silence. Sometimes sounds are introduced to cover other sounds, sometimes echoes are used to encourage silence, and sometimes acoustics weren't thought about at all and having a simple conversation becomes a frustrating experience.

In addition to using the sense to see the sights, meandering around looking for things to read is a good way to find more of a story as well. Plaques, names, dates, inscriptions, etc., could all be considered as pieces to a puzzle. Use these small pieces of reading in conjunction with the research done before the trip to build a broader picture of the significance of the destination.

Finally, don't underestimate the satisfaction of completing a quick sketch. Pictures are fantastic, pictures are quick, pictures are ever easier now that everyone carries a miniature camera in their pockets. However, a few sketches from the trip are a nice way to reminisce. There's something about the craft, that sense of hand-made pride that fills a sketch with so much life. Not only that, but sitting down in a public place and drawing something pen on paper is quite relaxing.

LOOKING BEYOND

I consider seeing the sights to differ from looking beyond in the same way that reading differs from reading between the lines. As I've mentioned relentlessly throughout this book, traveling like an architect requires searching for a story. What stories we search for are individual decisions, but nonetheless they must be found.

In this chapter, the concept of learning circles back around. Research was done before the trip to gain some background information on the destination, and now that comes into use. Now is the opportunity to visualize how those stories affected the architecture, to travel across time and feel the footsteps of those who once passed through the space. It's almost like a game, really, moving through a space and visualizing an event from the past like one of those detectives on television.

One clue leads to another in an exciting unfolding of observations, yet not every clue may be recognizable. Fret not, for this is the opportunity to take note for later. Yes, nothing could be more fantastic than discovering an unanswered question, for that means an opportunity to search for more articles, more books, more puzzle pieces to fit into the story and create a clearer picture.

But how, exactly, could a building or a city or a park have its line read between? Simple, look for what is on display and then focus on everything else. Even the shape of the air between the walls can paint a different picture. For instance, there are two bays of tile work in the Pantheon that differ from the rest; that is something worthy of research because there has to be a story explaining why. Really, anything that stands out from the rest of the architectural piece or looks quirky in any way has a story.

This concept applies to cities or landscapes, too, not just buildings. Ever notice a sea of parking lots in the downtown area of a city or an unusually large concentration of vacant lots in a neighborhood? It's possible there used to be buildings there. History and stories wiped from the visual experience and now only exist in the realm of the written word.

At the very core of the idea, looking beyond when traveling as an architect occupies the same brain function as imagination. Feel free to take a back seat to the inner child; let them run rampant searching for seemingly unimportant, unlikely places to ask "why" as children do so well. Stories happen everywhere and can be found revolving around anything.

NOTES

NOTES

NOTES

PART THREE

After the Trip

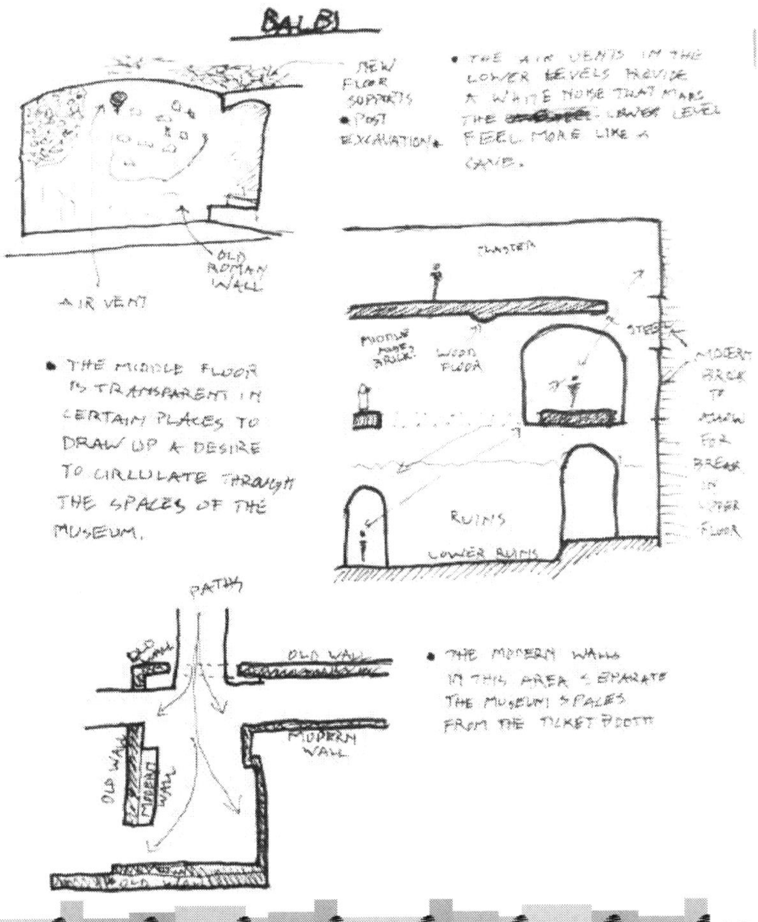

REFLECTING ON THE LESSONS

Returning home from a good trip can be disappointing. Not only (for longer trips) is work on Monday the typical next step, but also the anticipation of a getaway no longer captivates the daydreams of the wandering mind. Those thoughts, instead, tend to become replaced with feelings of self-resentment for not becoming a famous travel blogger overnight and living on royalty checks while backpacking around the globe.

So how then, can we reconcile with these emotions to fill our desperate need for daily positivity? The truth is--as I've stated numerous times in this book already--everybody operates differently and deals with their emotions in unique ways. Therefore, what I offer in this chapter are ways in which I've reflected on my time spent traveling but are far from the only ways.

Perhaps the most popular way to reflect on a longer trip is the art of scrap-booking. Varying from simple photo-books ordered online to elaborate amalgamations of cuttings, trimmings, and journal entries. No matter the format, flipping through photographs, putting the best ones in an orderly layout, and marveling at the finished product provides opportunities to reflect on the most memorable parts of the trip.

But, other forms of physical expression can be taken. I, as may be obvious, enjoy writing, but I'm not one to turn away from a nice painting either. Flowing feelings into artwork is a great way to get children involved in reflecting over a trip as well.

Visiting destinations with a much shorter travel distance, by contrast, has different opportunities for reflection. As a personal example, I made a destination out of the ATM at my bank back in the early days of the pandemic. To fully enjoy my out-of-the-house excursion to my campus corner bank, I decided to park on the opposite side of the university and walk a mile through campus to enjoy the architecture along the way. Upon returning home, I realized the trip was unparalleled in a mixture of both exercise and relaxation. Walking through a picturesque city-scape, sipping a cup of coffee, soaking in the sunshine, all the while free to let my mind wander. Quickly, this mini-vacation to the bank became a weekly adventure.

I bring this up as the best example i have of why traveling like an architect doesn't require an expensive, once-in-a-life-time outing. Architecture is everywhere, and learning to fall in love with the common, ordinary architecture that blends into the background gives a greater sense of fulfillment.

And of course, how could I not mention a bit more learning. What I've mentioned so far in terms of artwork and repeated travels along the same path do provide great chances for self-reflection and a personal form of learning. Still, there must be something said for the curiosities noted while on the trip, the unexpectedly captivating details that earned further investigation. Just as articles were read to prepare for traveling, now is the opportunity to search for articles or documentaries post-travel to look for those explanations of those details. Finding the fantasy within nonfiction makes it easier to digest.

PLANNING THE NEXT ONE

And almost as if the trip never happened in the first place, the urge to travel again kicks back in not a week later. The question then looms, does the next trip have any relation to the first or not? Certainly, starting fresh is a perfectly reasonable and valid way to plan the next trip, but oh, the possibilities of planning a sequel trip in an effort to continue the story of the first.

I must add before assumptions are made, a sequel trip does not necessarily mean traveling back to the same destination for a second time--with an exception to trips around town as I mentioned in the previous chapter. Though the nostalgia of such a trip would be sure to thrill, the excitement of falling in love with a new destination and broadening one's world view thrills plenty as well.

Choosing anything really can feel as stressful as someone saying "please say your name, major, and a fun fact about yourself," but it doesn't need to be as deep as I make it sound. After my trip to Rome, I decided to stop in Barcelona on my way home. Did I choose this location because I wanted to see the Barcelona Pavilion by Mies van der Rohe, which was an early example of the International Style I had seen around Rome? Yes. Did I choose Barcelona from a list of other cities because it was the cheapest flight option? Also yes. Planning should include an architectural reason, but don't forget that architecture is everywhere, and planning based on finances or personal circumstance is just as valid.

But in the end, traveling like an architect doesn't mean subscribing to any one set of rules or itinerary. The diversity in tastes and opinions in the architecture field is no different than any other career position. Moreover, each individual person will come into their own way of traveling like an architect as long as they commit to seeing the world as a puzzle.

So then, where should the next trip be planned? Yes, exactly. What comes later reveals itself once what will be was (this makes sense in my head). It's not so much about knowing where to go next as it is a feeling. After all, what are humans if not emotionally driven creatures. Get out there and see the world, and don't forget the world can be just around the block.

NOTES

NOTES

NOTES

WHAT'S NEXT

This may be hard to believe, but I wrote this book on a whim. I got bored during my post-graduation job hunt, and decided, hey, maybe instead of searching for a run-of-the-mill nine-to-five I could write a book and see if that could blossom into a career. Well, because I have yet to learn how to see into the future, I don't know whether or not this book will sell enough for that to happen.

Although, I have had a lot of fun writing this book. It became a great mental exercise for me to relive my own travel experiences and decipher not only what about them I found enjoyable, but also how they helped me to grow as an architectural scholar. The former unquestionably came easier than the latter, but that's not even mentioning the process of transcribing this book into a children's edition.

Currently, I have plans for at least one more book because any adventure is worthy of a sequel. This book will be within the same series "Travel like an Architect," but instead of describing abstract concepts, I plan to actually write in detail about a specific travel experience at a specific destination. More information on this next book is given on pages 62 and 63.

Potentially, this could continue into a whole travel series with multiple books covering multiple destinations. I feel, though, that the big destinations are covered extensively in a nauseating amount of travel guides and articles, so this series would focus on more overlooked and under-appreciated destinations for those looking to stand apart from the crowd in their journeys.

Yet as the ever experimental creative I am, I may hop around different genres in the future as well. Fiction books, photography books, poetry books, etc., are all on the table. I am a go-with-the-flow kind of person, so stay tuned if that kind of author captures intrigue.

NOTES

WHERE WILL YOU GO NOW?

TRAVEL LIKE AN ARCHITECT

GHOSTS OF SEGREGATION

BE ON THE LOOK OUT

This is the first book in a series in which I will travel to different cities and comment on the aspect of architecture that interests me most: socio-political. For example, my next book will be titled "Travel Like an Architect: Ghosts of Segregation," and I will discuss how the segregation, redlining, and gentrification of the black community can still be seen in the architecture of the Deep Deuce neighborhood in Oklahoma City. If that interests you, be sure to visit my website and subscribe to my newsletter to catch its release.

cevanh.myportfolio.com

C EVAN H

KIDS' EDITION

TRAVEL LIKE AN ARCHITECT

THE BASICS

HAVE LITTLE ONES? CHECK OUT THE KIDS EDITION OF THIS BOOK!

C EVAN H

ABOUT THE AUTHOR

C. Evan H. is a young graduate from the University of Oklahoma's Master of Architecture program. Though in his time there, he grew a passion for writing as much as he had for architecture. Like so many, he enjoys grabbing a cup of coffee and going on an adventure, whether that be across the world or to the grocery store. Learn more about him on his website:

cevanh.myportfolio.com

THANKS FOR READING!

Follow me on Instagram for updates on future books

C_EVAN_H_

Made in the USA
Columbia, SC
28 August 2021

44153163R00041